cocktail

guide

Cole's Home Library Cookbooks
Glen Ellen, California

cocktail guide

Few can resist a tantalizing cocktail and our selection of palate pleasers will make the task even more difficult! We have divided the cocktails into four sections, indicating the time of day when they are most suitable to serve. Remember though, a cocktail can taste great at any time! Within the sections the cocktails are listed under the main ingredient, e.g. Tequila-based or non-alcoholic, and all cocktails serve one person unless specified otherwise. We have also advised in which glass the cocktail is traditionally served and the accompanying garnish, but the final choice is yours. Experiment with glassware, garnishes and cocktails to fit in with the mood of your gathering.

Left to right: pink gin, blue riband and evergreen, page 92

Irish coffee, page 120

Grand Marnier fireball, page 110

Silver sunset and Long Island tea, page 39

Hot toddy, page 113

contents

essential equipment

Many of the items may already be in your kitchen cupboard; the rest can easily be found in department stores or specialty shops.

Blender A very useful cocktail bar item. It should have several speed selections and be able to crush ice. The blender should be kept scrupulously clean. (1)

Bottle opener For beer bottles, any soft drink bottles or mixers without screw tops. (2)

Bowls For olives, sugar, garnishes. (3)

Chopping board On which to cut fruit. (4)

Corkscrew To open wine or other corked bottles. (5)

Grater For grating chocolate or nutmeg. (6)

Hawthorn strainer A wire strainer which traps the ice but allows the liquid to pass through. It has an edge of rolled wire to prevent spillage. (7)

Ice bucket For storing the ice to be used for drinks. (8)

Ice scoop For getting ice for drinks. (9)

Juice extractor Useful for making fresh fruit juice. (10)

Knife For chopping fruit. (11)

Measures (also called pourers, tots and jiggers), necessary to measure exact amount of ingredients. Most useful measures are 1/2 oz and 1 oz. (12)

Pitcher Should have lips to hold back the ice, and be large enough to hold lots of ice. (13)

Sealers For mixer bottles and champagne bottles that have been opened and still have liquid left in them. (14)

Shaker Consisting of two cones, one glass and one metal, it is highly recommended, or a shaker with a built-in strainer. Make sure the lid is secure before shaking. (15)

Spoons The long-handled ones are the most useful for stirring. The handle should not be smooth as it may become slippery when wet; many of the spoons available have a spiral pattern on handle. (16)

Tongs For fruit or ice. (17)

Tos or zester To get zest from fruit peel. (18)

Other equipment you will need:

Mixing glass Used to stir cocktails and ensure the drink is served cold. A glass pitcher can be used. Should hold between 1 pint and 1 quart and have lips.

Stirrers or swizzle sticks, straws, toothpicks, napkins, coasters and cloths.

glasses

The glasses in which you serve your cocktails are every bit as important as the ingredients, the taste and the garnishes. Our recipes tell you in which glass the cocktail is traditionally served but the final choice is yours. Allow room for a generous amount of drink and garnishes.

Make sure the glass is completely free of any detergent or odor (if glasses are stored upside-down the air trapped in the bowl will become stale and affect the taste and smell of the drink); rinse these glasses before using.

If you have a large refrigerator or freezer it's a good idea to chill your glasses before using them. As well as being attractive, it keeps the drink chilled just that little bit longer.

Wash and rinse glasses in very hot water, then dry with one cloth and polish them with another.

Use real glass and not plastic glasses so as not to affect the taste of the drink. Remember too, that multicolored designs on glasses tend to detract from the drink you are serving.

Cocktail glass A V-shaped or triangular glass used for short, strong drinks. It should have a long stem to keep the cocktail chilled as long as possible. If the bowl of the glass is held in a warm hand, the hand becomes wet and the cocktail will lose its chill. Holds about 3 oz. (**1**)

Champagne glass Either a saucer or a flute shape. The long tapering flute (**2**) allows bubbles to rise in a continuous stream. Holds about 5 oz. The saucer (**3**) is not as popular as it once was for champagne drinks as the bubbles disappear quickly, it is however still favored for some cocktails such as the Margarita, Bartender and creamy drinks.

Highball A tall straight-sided glass used mainly for long drinks with ice – anything from a lemonade or a Mai-Tai to a beer. Holds about 6–10 oz. (**4**)

Old-fashioned A tumbler with traditionally sloping sides used mainly for spirits with ice, short unstrained drinks or fruit juices. Holds about 4 oz. (**5**)

Stemmed wine glasses Available in a variety of shapes and sizes. Red wine is best served in a larger glass while white wine is suited to a smaller glass. Suitable for a range of exotic cocktails. Holds about 5–6 oz. (**6**)

Brandy balloon (not pictured) Designed so that the full aroma of the brandy can be savored, but cocktails can look spectacular in these glasses. Should hold not more than 5 oz.

mixing a cocktail

It takes years of practice to achieve a perfectly mixed cocktail, but with a few simple rules in mind you can create some sensational taste combinations.

Before mixing a drink, have everything required close at hand and do as much as possible in advance. Use quality products when mixing drinks and always follow recipes accurately. Measuring ingredients exactly is important if the drink is to have the right consistency. Prepare lots of fresh ice and have it ready for use, cut fruit into cubes and also check that your glassware is clean and in good order before guests arrive.

Serving food with cocktails will pace your guests' alcoholic intake and avoid mixing too many different spirits. The best drinks use one spirit as a base and have simple uncomplicated flavors. Use garnishes to add decoration and give an extra complimentary taste of the drink.

Some recipes may sound daunting if they mention too many different terms. Here are a few of the more common that may be encountered.

Float ingredients A technique usually done after a cocktail has been made. A spoon is rested on the top of the drink and the liquid poured into its dish until the spoon is filled; the ingredients flow over it and onto the surface of the drink.

Muddling refers to the use of the back of the spoon (or special muddler) to mash aromatic ingredients together (e.g. sugar cubes or mint leaves) to blend them and release the desired flavors and aromas.

Frosting is the technique where sugar or salt is used to coat the rim of a glass. To do this, hold the glass upside-down by the stem, rub a slice of lemon around the rim, then dip the glass into the sugar or salt and leave to dry. To achieve a colored effect on the rim, place a little grenadine or colored liqueur into a plate and coat the rim of the glass with it before dipping it in the sugar or salt.

Cocktails can be shaken, stirred, blended or built. These four methods of mixing are the most popular.

1 To shake a cocktail is to mix it in a cocktail shaker by hand, making sure to fill the shaker three-quarters full with ice first. Pour the ingredients in on top of the ice. Cocktails that include ingredients such as egg whites, fresh juice and cream should be shaken for about 10 seconds, then strained into a cocktail glass.

2 Stirred cocktails are mixed by stirring with ice in a mixing glass until cold, and are then strained into a cocktail glass.

3 Blended cocktails are mixed using an electric blender. Fresh fruit or fresh juices and alcohol are mixed well using this method. Add crushed ice if recipe requires and blend long enough for it to be mixed with the liquid to reach the desired consistency; it should be smooth.

4 Building a cocktail refers to mixing the ingredients in the glass they will be served in. The ingredients are floated on top of each other and swizzle sticks can be placed in the glass to allow the ingredients to be mixed.

A few more points to remember when mixing cocktails are:

◆ Always use good quality products.

◆ Juices should be at least 50 per cent pure juice or they will water the cocktail down.

◆ After the canned ingredients are opened, transfer them to clean bottles so they keep longer.

Measurements of certain quantities are also useful to know when mixing drinks. The ones most often encountered are:

◆ A dash = 10 drops = 1/4 teaspoon

◆ 1 jigger = 1 pony = 1 oz = 30ml

◆ Miniature = 1.6 oz = 50ml

◆ 1 wine glass = 4 oz = 125ml

Other cocktail terms:

Frappe to serve a cocktail over finely crushed ice.

Flip a drink made with eggs.

Mulls hot wine punch.

Punch mixed spirits or wines with spices, fruit juices and sugar. May be served hot or cold.

ice

Ice is used in nearly all cocktails so it is important to have clean, fresh cubes, blocks or crushed ice. Remember, a warm cocktail is, quite simply, undrinkable.

Well iced drinks are best because they have more body; the ice improves the texture by thickening the drink. It is important, however, to always add the ice first so it chills the liquid quickly and thoroughly and doesn't overflow the glass.

Prepare ice in the size and shape desired then place in the freezer for about 30 minutes to re-freeze it; melting ice is of little use.

Cubed ice can be prepared in freezer trays in many different sizes, and can be crushed easily. Crush ice cubes by wrapping them in a tea towel then hitting it on a wall or floor, or with a hammer or rolling pin. Electric and hand-operated ice crushers are also available.

For ice cubes with a difference, place lemon wedges, fruit pieces or olive slices in water in ice tray. Allow to freeze, use in cocktails.

tequila-based

blue monday

1 oz tequila
1 oz Drambuie
1 oz blue curaçao
lemonade
ice

Pour tequila, Drambuie, curaçao and ice into shaker, shake, then pour into serving glass. Top with lemonade.

glass 10 oz highball

garnish lemon and orange slice and a cherry

It is served in the afternoon.

right blue monday

eye openers

Enticing drinks to awaken both you and your appetite. Choose from bubbling champagne delights, refreshingly fruity non-alcoholic mixtures or other spirited concoctions, then all that's left to do is sit back and enjoy an unhurried breakfast as ceiling fans whir overhead and the perfume of the blossoms fill the air. What a great thought to wake up to!

brandy-based

morning glory

10 oz brandy
1/2 oz orange curaçao
1/2 oz pure lemon juice
dash Angostura bitters
dash Pernod
ice

Pour all ingredients into shaker, shake, then strain into serving glass.

glass 3 oz cocktail glass

garnish lemon twist

right morning glory

brandy-based

corpse reviver

1 oz brandy
1/2 oz Calvados
1/2 oz rosso vermouth
ice

Pour all ingredients into shaker, shake, then strain into serving glass.

glass 3 oz cocktail glass

garnish none

eggnog

1/2 oz sugar syrup
1 oz brandy
1 oz dark rum
1 egg
ice
3 oz milk

Pour sugar syrup, brandy, rum, egg and ice into blender, blend, pour into serving glass then top up with milk. Stir.

glass 10 oz highball

garnish nutmeg and a cherry

right eggnog

below corpse reviver

brandy-based

prairie oyster

1 egg yolk
salt to taste
pepper to taste
dash Worcestershire sauce
2 drops Tabasco
1 oz brandy (optional)

Pour ingredients into serving glass, one
after the other. Preferably, do not stir,
but swallow in one gulp. We cheated a
little and stirred ours to make it look
more desirable!

glass   3 oz cocktail glass

garnish   none

champagne-based

mimosa

2 tsp orange curaçao
1 oz fresh orange juice
chilled champagne

Pour curaçao and juice into glass and top
with champagne.

glass   4 oz champagne flute

garnish   orange twist

left prairie oyster

right mimosa

beer-based

red eye

chilled beer
tomato juice

Pour equal quantities of ingredients into beer glass.

glass beer glass

garnish none

below red eye

vodka-based

perfect love

1 oz vodka
1/2 oz Parfait Amour
1/2 oz maraschino
ice

Pour ingredients, one after the other, into serving glass filled with ice.

glass 5 oz old-fashioned

garnish lemon twist

right perfect love

vodka-based

bloody mary

1 oz vodka
salt or celery salt
pepper
dash Tabasco sauce
dash Worcestershire sauce
dash lemon juice
ice
4 oz tomato juice

Pour vodka, salt, pepper, Tabasco sauce, Worcestershire sauce and lemon juice over ice in serving glass. Stir with swizzle stick. Add tomato juice and stir with swizzle stick.

glass 10 oz highball

garnish lemon wedge and stick of crisp celery

quiet sunday

1 oz vodka
¹/₂ oz amaretto
4 oz fresh orange juice
¹/₂ egg white
ice
grenadine

Pour vodka, amaretto, orange juice, egg white and ice into serving glass. Splash grenadine into glass last.

glass 10 oz highball

garnish orange ring and cherry

left bloody mary

right quiet sunday

vodka-based

bullshot

1 oz vodka
4 oz beef stock
1¹/₂ tsp lemon juice
dash Worcestershire sauce
pinch celery salt
pepper to taste
ice

Pour all ingredients into shaker, shake,
then strain into serving glass.

glass 10 oz highball

garnish slice of lemon

sherry-based

sherry flip

2 oz cream sherry
1 egg
ice

Pour all ingredients into blender,
blend until smooth, then pour into
serving glass.

glass 5 oz wine glass

garnish sprinkle of nutmeg

left bullshot

right sherry flip

bourbon-based

mint julep

5 mint leaves
1 tsp sugar syrup
1 tsp water
ice
2 oz bourbon

Crush mint leaves in glass with sugar
syrup and water to extract mint flavor.
Add ice and bourbon. Stir for
30 seconds until glass frosts.

glass 6 oz highball

garnish mint leaves

non-alcoholic

fruit fantasy

4 oz fresh orange juice
2 oz pineapple juice
6 strawberries
small slice honeydew melon
small slice cantaloupe
ice

Pour all ingredients into blender, blend
until smooth, pour into serving glass.

glass 10 oz highball

garnish fruit in season

left *mint julep*

below *fruit fantasy*

non-alcoholic

pussyfoot

2 oz fresh orange juice
1 oz fresh lemon juice
1 oz fresh lime juice
dash grenadine
1 egg yolk
ice

Pour all ingredients into shaker, shake, then pour into serving glass.

glass 10 oz highball

garnish orange slice and cherry

cinderella

2 oz orange juice
2 oz pineapple juice
2 oz fresh lemon juice
ice

Pour all ingredients into shaker, shake, then pour into serving glass.

glass 10 oz highball

garnish fruit in season

left *pussyfoot*
below left *cinderella*   ***below right*** *pom pom*

pom pom

1 oz fresh lemon juice
1/2 egg white
1 tsp grenadine
chilled lemonade
ice

Pour juice, egg white and grenadine into shaker, shake, then strain into serving glass. Top with lemonade and ice, pouring slowly.

glass 10 oz highball

garnish lemon slice and cherry

afternoon delights

During Prohibition in the 1920s, adventurous drinkers began mixing bits and pieces together to disguise the taste of their poor-quality liquor. We have followed the lead with gusto, although we don't need to cover the taste anymore, and today there is a tantalizing range of cocktails, some just perfect for sipping in the lazy afternoon. Try an icy Frozen Daiquiri, celebrate with a Rhett Butler, float away on a Barrier Reef, enjoy a Long Island Tea or introduce yourself to a Fluffy Duck.

rum-based

blossom

1¹/₂ oz light rum
¹/₂ oz fresh orange juice
¹/₂ oz fresh lemon juice
¹/₂ oz sugar syrup
ice

Pour all ingredients into shaker, shake, then strain into serving glass.

glass 4 oz champagne saucer

garnish orange and a cherry

el dorado

1 oz light rum
1 oz advocaat
1 oz white crème de cacao
1 oz cream of coconut
ice

Rub rim of glass with orange slice, dip rim into coconut to coat. Pour all ingredients into shaker, shake, strain into serving glass.

glass 10 oz highball

garnish orange slices and cherries

left from left, blossom, el dorado

rum-based

casablanca

1½ oz light rum
3 oz pineapple juice
1 oz cream of coconut
½ oz grenadine
ice

Pour all ingredients into blender, blend until smooth, then pour into a serving glass.

glass 10 oz highball

garnish pineapple and a cherry

planter's punch

2 oz light rum
1 oz fresh orange juice
1 oz fresh lime juice
1 tsp grenadine
dash of Angostura bitters
ice
soda water

Pour rum, juices, grenadine and bitters into serving glass filled with ice. Top with soda water and mix.

glass 10 oz highball glass

garnish orange, lime and lemon slices, and cherries

below casablanca   *right* planter's punch

rum-based

blue hawaii

1 oz light rum
¹/₂ oz amaretto
¹/₂ oz blue curaçao
¹/₂ oz Rose's lime juice
3 oz pineapple juice
ice

Pour all ingredients into shaker, shake, then pour into serving glass.

glass 10 oz highball

garnish pineapple spear and a cherry

pina colada

1 oz light rum
4 oz pineapple juice
1 oz cream of coconut (or Malibu)
¹/₂ oz sugar syrup
ice

Pour all ingredients into blender, blend until smooth, then pour into serving glass.

glass 10 oz highball

garnish pineapple leaves and a cherry

mai-tai

1 oz light rum
¹/₂ oz amaretto
¹/₂ oz orange curaçao
¹/₂ oz lemon juice
¹/₂ oz sugar syrup
1 oz dark rum
lime shell, squeezed
ice

Pour ingredients, one on top of the other, into serving glass filled with ice, stir gently with swizzle stick.

glass 10 oz highball

garnish pineapple spear, leaves, cherry

left *from left, blue hawaii, pina colada*

right *mai-tai*

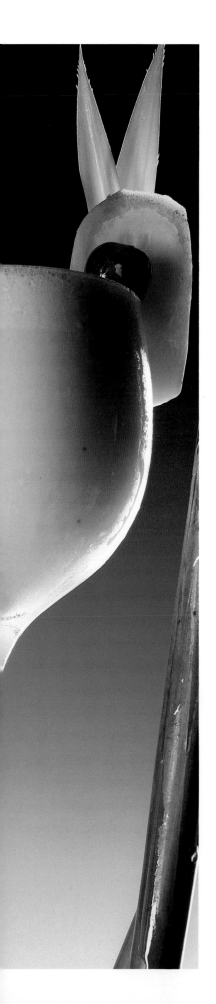

rum-based

strawberry daiquiri

4 ripe strawberries
1 oz light rum
1 oz Cointreau
1 oz lemon juice
ice

Pour all ingredients into blender, blend, then strain into serving glass.

glass 5 oz champagne saucer

garnish strawberry

banana colada

1 oz light rum
1 oz cream of coconut
1 oz sugar syrup
1 oz fresh cream
4 oz pineapple juice
1/2 banana
ice

Pour all ingredients into blender, blend, then pour into serving glass.

glass 10 oz fancy

garnish banana, pineapple and
                  mint leaves

yellow bird

1 1/2 oz light rum
3/4 oz Galliano
3/4 oz Cointreau
3/4 oz fresh lime juice
ice

Pour all ingredients into shaker, shake, then pour into serving glass.

glass 6 oz old-fashioned

garnish slice of lime in drink

left from left, strawberry daiquiri, banana colada
below yellow bird

rum-based

sarah jane

1 oz light rum
1/2 oz Grand Marnier
1/2 oz apricot brandy
1 oz orange juice
1 oz fresh cream
11/2 tsp Galliano
ice

Pour all ingredients into shaker, shake, then strain into serving glass.

glass 5 oz champagne saucer

garnish chocolate flake, a strawberry

fluffy duck

1 oz light rum
1 oz advocaat
ice
lemonade
cream

Pour rum and advocaat into serving glass filled with ice and top with lemonade, mix well. Pour cream over a spoon so it overflows the spoon and floats on the surface of the drink.

glass 10 oz highball

garnish strawberry

frozen daiquiri

11/2 oz light rum
1 oz fresh lemon juice
1/2 oz sugar syrup
2 scoops of ice

Pour all ingredients into blender, blend until smooth, then pour into serving glass.

glass 5 oz champagne saucer

garnish lemon slice

left *from left, sarah jane, fluffy duck, frozen daiquiri*

rum-based

blue heaven

1 oz light rum
1/2 oz amaretto
1/2 oz blue curaçao
1/2 oz fresh lime juice
21/2 oz pineapple juice
ice

Pour all ingredients into shaker, shake, then pour into serving glass.

glass 10 oz highball

garnish pineapple piece, leaves
             and a cherry

vodka-based

screwdriver

2 oz vodka
2 oz fresh orange juice
ice

Pour ingredients, one after the other, into serving glass filled with ice.

glass 5 oz old-fashioned

garnish orange slice

harvey wallbanger

1 oz vodka
4 oz orange juice
1/2 oz Galliano
ice

Pour ingredients, one after the other, into serving glass filled with ice.
Stir with a swizzle stick if desired.

glass 10 oz highball

garnish orange slice and a cherry

left *blue heaven*   **right** *screwdriver*

vodka-based

long island tea

1 oz vodka
1 oz tequila
1 oz light rum
1/2 oz Cointreau
1/2 oz fresh lemon juice
1/2 oz sugar syrup
1 oz cola
ice

Pour all ingredients, one after the other, into serving glass filled with ice. Stir with a swizzle stick.

glass 10 oz highball
garnish lemon twist and mint leaves

salty dog

1 1/2 oz vodka
4 oz fresh grapefruit juice
ice

Rub rim of glass with lemon slice then dip into salt, to coat the rim. Pour all ingredients, one after the other, into the salted glass filled with ice.

glass 10 oz highball
garnish lemon twist

silver sunset

1 oz vodka
1/2 oz apricot brandy
1/2 oz Campari
3 oz fresh orange juice
1/2 egg white
ice

Pour all ingredients into shaker, shake, then pour into serving glass.

glass 10 oz highball
garnish orange slice and cherry

right *from left, salty dog, silver sunset, long island tea*
below *harvey wallbanger (recipe previous page)*

tequila-based

vesuvius

1 oz tequila
4 oz orange juice
¹/₂ oz Campari
ice

Pour ingredients, one after the other, over ice into serving glass.

glass 10 oz highball

garnish orange spiral

acapulco

1 oz tequila
1 oz Tia Maria
1 oz dark rum
1 oz pineapple juice
1 oz cream of coconut
ice

Pour all ingredients into shaker, shake, then pour into serving glass.

glass 10 oz highball

garnish pineapple slice and leaves, and a cherry

viva mexico

1 oz tequila
³/₄ oz white crème de cacao
³/₄ oz Midori melon liqueur
1 oz pineapple juice
1 oz orange juice
ice

Pour all ingredients into shaker, shake, then pour into serving glass.

glass 10 oz highball

garnish slice of orange and a cherry

right *from left, vesuvius, acapulco, viva mexico*

tequila-based

brave bull

1 oz tequila
1 oz Kahlua
ice

Pour ingredients, one after the other, into serving glass filled with ice, stir if desired.

glass 4 oz old-fashioned

garnish none

tequila sunrise

1 oz tequila
4 oz orange juice
1¹/₂ tsp grenadine
ice

Pour tequila and orange juice, one after the other, over ice in serving glass. Drop grenadine through center of cocktail.

glass 10 oz highball

garnish orange slice and a maraschino cherry

right tequila sunrise   ***below*** *brave bull*

brandy-based

brandy highball

dash Angostura bitters
1 oz brandy
chilled soda water (or dry ginger ale)
ice

Coat inside of glass with bitters,
add brandy. Top with soda water
or dry ginger ale.

glass 10 oz highball

garnish lemon spiral

southerly buster

1 oz brandy
1/2 oz dry vermouth
1/2 oz Rose's lime juice
dry ginger ale
ice

Pour brandy, dry vermouth and Rose's
lime juice into serving glass filled with ice.
Top with dry ginger ale.

glass 10 oz highball.

garnish lemon slice.

below *from left, brandy highball, southerly buster*

rum-based

coconut breeze

1 oz dark rum
1 oz pineapple juice
1 oz cream of coconut
1¹/₂ tsp maraschino
1¹/₂ tsp amaretto
ice

Pour all ingredients into shaker, shake, then pour into serving glass.

glass 5 oz champagne saucer

garnish sprinkle with grated coconut

love in the afternoon

1 oz dark rum
1 oz fresh orange juice
1 oz cream of coconut
¹/₂ oz sugar syrup
¹/₂ oz fresh cream
5 strawberries
ice

Pour all ingredients into blender, blend until smooth, then strain into serving glass.

glass 6 oz old-fashioned

garnish chocolate flake and a strawberry

right black velvet

below *from left, coconut breeze, love in the afternoon*

44

beer-based

black velvet

stout beer
champagne

Pour equal quantities of ingredients into serving glass. Stir if desired.

glass champagne flute

garnish none

gin-based

blue lagoon

1 oz gin or vodka
4 oz lemonade
1 oz blue curaçao
ice

Pour ingredients, one after the other, into serving glass filled with ice, stir with swizzle stick if desired.

glass 10 oz highball

garnish orange slice and cherry

negroni

³/₄ oz gin
³/₄ oz rosso vermouth
³/₄ oz Campari
soda water (optional)
ice

Pour ingredients, one after the other, into serving glass filled with ice.

glass 10 oz highball

garnish orange slice

raffles singapore sling

dash Angostura bitters
1 oz gin
¹/₂ oz Triple Sec
¹/₂ oz Benedictine
¹/₂ oz cherry brandy
¹/₂ oz fresh lime juice
1 oz pineapple juice
1 oz fresh orange juice
ice

Pour all ingredients, one after the other, into serving glass filled with ice, stir gently with swizzle stick.

glass 10 oz highball.

garnish orange slice and a cherry

right *from left, blue lagoon, negroni*
far right *raffles singapore sling*

46

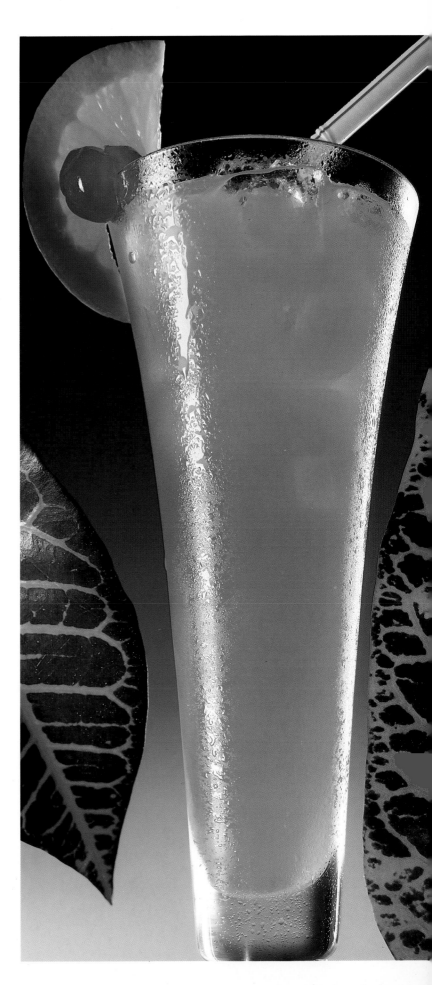

gin-based

caribbean sunset

1 oz gin
1 oz banana liqueur
1 oz blue curaçao
1 oz fresh lemon juice
1 oz fresh cream
ice
dash of grenadine

Pour gin, banana liqueur, blue curaçao,
lemon juice and cream into shaker with
ice, shake, strain into serving glass.
Add grenadine.

glass 10 oz cocktail glass

garnish fruit in season

barrier reef

2 oz gin
1 oz Cointreau
dash Angostura bitters
2 scoops vanilla ice-cream
dash blue curaçao
ice

Pour all ingredients into shaker,
shake, then pour into serving glass.

glass 10 oz highball

garnish pineapple slice and leaves

blue bayou

1 oz gin
1/2 oz Galliano
1/2 oz dry vermouth
1/2 oz blue curaçao
lemonade
ice

Pour gin, Galliano, vermouth and curaçao
into shaker, shake, then pour into serving
glass. Top with lemonade and ice.

glass 10 oz highball

garnish lemon wheel and mint leaves

left caribbean sunset

right from left, barrier reef, blue bayou

gin-based

south pacific

1 oz gin
¹/₂ oz Galliano
ice
lemonade
¹/₂ oz blue curaçao

Pour gin and Galliano into serving glass filled with ice, top with lemonade. Splash blue curaçao through the drink; it will sink to the bottom of the drink.

glass 10 oz highball

garnish lemon slice

moon river

1 oz gin
1 oz apricot brandy
1 oz Cointreau
¹/₂ oz Galliano
¹/₂ oz fresh lime juice
ice

Pour all ingredients into shaker, shake, then pour into serving glass.

glass 10 oz highball

garnish orange or lemon slice, and cherry

whisky-based

crazy horse

1 oz scotch whisky
¹/₂ oz strawberry liqueur
¹/₂ oz crème de banane
ice
chilled champagne

Pour scotch whisky, strawberry liqueur, crème de banane and ice into shaker, shake, then strain into serving glass. Top with champagne.

glass 6 oz champagne flute

garnish orange and lime slices, strawberries and mint leaves

left from left, south pacific, moon river

right crazy horse

whisky-based

old-fashioned

1 sugar cube
Angostura bitters
1 oz soda water
ice
2 oz scotch whisky or bourbon

Soak sugar cube with bitters and place into serving glass. Cover cube with soda water, crush and mix to dissolve cube. Add ice, stir, then add scotch whisky.

glass 6 oz old-fashioned

garnish orange and lemon slices, and a cherry

wine-based

sangria

1 bottle red wine
1 oz Cointreau
1 oz light rum
1 oz brandy
1/2 cup sugar
ice

Pour ingredients into a large pitcher filled with ice, stir well until combined, then pour into serving glasses.

glass 5 oz wine goblet

garnish orange, lemon and strawberry pieces

spritzer

chilled white wine
chilled soda water

Pour equal quantities of ingredients into serving glass.

glass 6 oz wine goblet

garnish none

left old-fashioned ***above*** sangria ***right*** spritzer

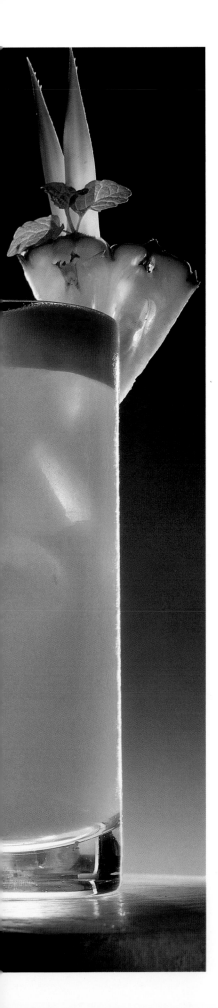

galliano-based

cantaloupe dream

1 oz Galliano
3/4 oz maraschino
1 oz fresh orange juice
1 oz fresh cream
3 scoops cantaloupe
ice

Pour all ingredients into blender, blend until smooth, then pour into serving glass.

glass 5 oz champagne glass

garnish cantaloupe balls

bossa nova

1 oz Galliano
1 oz light rum
1/2 oz apricot brandy
1/2 oz fresh lemon juice
1 oz pineapple juice
dash egg white
ice

Pour all ingredients into shaker, shake, then pour into serving glass.

glass 10 oz highball

garnish pineapple slice and leaves, mint

left from left, cantaloupe dream, bossa nova
below peach marnier (recipe over page)

curaçao-based

rhett butler

1 oz orange curaçao
1 oz Southern Comfort
1/2 oz fresh lemon juice
1/2 oz fresh lime juice
ice
soda water

Pour curaçao, Southern Comfort, juices and ice into shaker, shake, then pour into serving glass. Top with soda water.

glass 10 oz highball

garnish orange slice and mint leaves

banana-liqueur-based

white gold

1 oz banana liqueur
1 oz Galliano
1 oz pineapple juice
1 oz apricot nectar
1/2 egg white
ice

Pour all ingredients into blender, blend until smooth, then pour into serving glass half-filled with ice.

glass 10 oz highball

garnish cherry and pineapple piece

malibu-based

french blue

1 oz Malibu
1/2 oz strawberry liqueur
1/4 banana
1/2 oz blue curaçao
ice

Pour all ingredients into blender, blend until smooth, then pour into serving glass.

glass 5 oz champagne saucer

garnish strawberries and banana slices

grand-marnier-based

peach marnier

1 oz Grand Marnier
1 oz dark rum
1 oz pineapple juice
1 oz sugar syrup
2 canned peach halves
ice

Pour all ingredients into blender blend until smooth, then pour into serving glass.

glass 6 oz old-fashioned

garnish peach slice and a cherry

right rhett butler
far right from left, french blue, white gold

57

southern-comfort-based

kelly's comfort

1 oz Southern Comfort
1 oz Baileys Irish Cream
2 oz milk
4 strawberries
1/2 oz sugar syrup
ice

Pour all ingredients into blender, blend until smooth, them pour into serving glass.

glass 10 oz highball

garnish strawberry

pernod polynesian

1 oz Southern Comfort
1/2 oz Pernod
2 oz orange and mango juice
1 oz fresh cream
ice
1/2 oz blue curaçao

Pour Southern Comfort, Pernod, juice, cream and ice into shaker, shake, then pour into serving glass. Drop blue curacao through drink; it will sink to the bottom of the drink.

glass 10 oz highball

garnish orange slice and cherry

far right el burro
below *from left, kelly's comfort, pernod polynesian*

kahlua-based

el burro

1/2 oz Kahlua
1/2 oz dark rum
1 oz cream of coconut
1 oz fresh cream
1/2 banana
ice

Pour all ingredients into blender, blend until smooth, then pour into serving glass.

glass 6 oz old-fashioned

garnish banana slice and mint leaves

kahlua-based

B52

1 oz Kahlua
1 oz Baileys Irish Cream
1 oz Cointreau
ice

Pour ingredients, one after the other, into serving glass filled with ice and stir with swizzle stick.

glass 6 oz old-fashioned

garnish none

white russian

1 oz Kahlua
1 oz vodka
1 oz fresh cream
ice

Pour ingredients, one after the other, over ice in serving glass, and stir with swizzle stick.

glass 6 oz old-fashioned

garnish none

tia-maria-based

lazy daze

1 oz Tia Maria
1/2 oz vodka
1 oz green crème de menthe
ice
lemonade
fresh cream

Pour Tia Maria, vodka, and crème de menthe into serving glass filled with ice. Top with lemonade, stir. Pour cream over a spoon so it overflows and floats on the surface.

glass 10 oz highball

garnish cherry and mint leaves

left B52
above *white russian*

right *lazy daze*

ouzo-based

jelly bean

1 oz ouzo
¹/₂ oz blue curaçao
¹/₂ oz grenadine
ice
lemonade

Pour ouzo, blue curaçao and grenadine
into serving glass filled with ice.
Top with lemonade.

glass 10 oz highball

garnish jelly bean

hot aphrodite

³/₄ oz ouzo
1 oz Vandermint
³/₄ oz green crème de menthe
³/₄ oz fresh cream
ice

Pour all ingredients into shaker, shake,
then strain into serving glass.

glass 5 oz champagne saucer

garnish black grapes and mint leaves

left jelly bean
below hot aphrodite
above touch of zam (recipe over page)

sambuca-based

touch of zam

³/₄ **oz Sambuca**
³/₄ **oz Benedictine**
³/₄ **oz Glayva**
1 oz orange juice
¹/₂ **oz fresh lemon juice**
ice

Pour all ingredients into shaker,
shake, then strain into serving glass.

glass 5 oz champagne saucer

garnish orange and lemon slices

apricot-brandy-based

champagne charlie

**¹/₂ oz apricot brandy
chilled champagne**

Pour apricot brandy into serving glass.
Top with champagne.

glass 6 oz champagne flute

garnish orange slice

pernod-based

death in the afternoon

**³/₄ oz Pernod
chilled champagne**

Pour Pernod into serving glass.
Top with chilled champagne.

glass 6 oz champagne flute

garnish none

midori-based

island affair

**1 oz Midori melon liqueur
¹/₂ oz Cointreau
¹/₂ oz blue curaçao
4 oz orange and mango juice
1 oz cream of coconut
ice**

Pour ingredients, one after the other,
into serving glass filled with ice.
Stir with swizzle stick of desired.

glass 10 oz highball

garnish slice of pineapple and a cherry

*left from left, champagne charlie,
death in the afternoon*

advocaat-based

dizzy blonde

2 oz advocaat
1 oz Pernod
ice
lemonade

Pour advocaat and Pernod into serving glass filled with ice. Top with lemonade.

glass 10 oz highball

garnish maraschino cherry

fallen angel

1 oz advocaat
1 oz cherry advocaat
ice
lemonade

Pour advocaat and cherry advocaat into serving glass filled with ice. Top with lemonade. Stir well.

glass 10 oz highball

garnish maraschino cherry

left *island affair (recipe previous page)*
right *from left, dizzy blonde, fallen angel*

non-alcoholic

passion

1 banana
2 oz pineapple juice
2 oz orange and mango juice
3 teaspoons passionfruit pulp
ice

Pour all ingredients into blender, blend until smooth, then pour into serving glass.

glass 10 oz highball

garnish banana and pineapple slices

right from left, surfers paradise, shirley temple
below from left, passion, cairns cooler

cairns cooler

2 oz pineapple juice
2 oz fresh orange juice
1 oz cream of coconut
1/2 oz sugar syrup
ice

Pour ingredients, one after the other, into serving glass filled with ice.

glass 10 oz highball

garnish pineapple slice and leaves, and a cherry

surfers paradise

1 oz fresh lime juice
2 dashes Angostura bitters
ice
lemonade

Pour lime juice and bitters, one after the other, over ice in serving glass. Top with lemonade.

glass 10 oz highball

garnish orange slice

shirley temple

1 oz grenadine
ice
lemonade
fresh cream

Pour grenadine over ice in serving glass. Top with lemonade and mix well. Float fresh cream on top.

glass 10 oz highball

garnish maraschino cherry

pre-dinner drinks

Cocktails are the perfect lead-in to dinner. Traditionally the martini – sweet, dry or medium – has occupied pride of place, but the choices are endless. Opt for a sparkling Kir Royale, a brandy-based Sidecar, a smooth Whisky Sour or a zesty Margarita to get your evening off to a tasty start.

bourbon-based

french 95

1/2 oz bourbon
1/2 oz fresh lemon juice
1/2 oz sugar syrup
ice
chilled champagne

Pour bourbon, lemon juice and sugar syrup into shaker with ice, shake, then strain into serving glass. Top with champagne.

glass 5 oz champagne flute
garnish lemon spiral

campari-based

americano

1 oz Campari
1 oz rosso vermouth
ice
soda water

Pour Campari then vermouth into serving glass filled with ice. Top with soda water, stir if desired.

glass 6 oz old-fashioned
garnish orange wheel and lemon spiral

ouzo-based

blue negligee

3/4 oz ouzo
3/4 oz Parfait Amour
3/4 oz green chartreuse
ice

Pour all ingredients into shaker, shake, then strain into serving glass.

glass 3 oz cocktail glass
garnish maraschino cherry

right *from left, french 95, americano, blue negligee*

vodka-based

vodka martini

1¹/₂ oz vodka
¹/₂ oz dry vermouth
ice

Pour all ingredients into mixing glass filled with ice, stir, then strain into serving glass.

glass 3 oz cocktail glass

garnish lemon twist

kamikaze

1 oz vodka
1 oz Cointreau
1 oz lemon juice
1 tsp Rose's lime juice
ice

Pour all ingredients into shaker, shake, then strain into serving glass.

glass 5 oz champagne saucer

garnish red cocktail onion

left vodka martini   *right* kamikaze

vodka-based

blue balalaika

¾ oz vodka
¾ oz Cointreau
¾ oz blue curaçao
¾ oz fresh lemon juice
ice

Pour all ingredients into shaker, shake, then strain into serving glass.

glass 3 oz cocktail glass

garnish lemon twist

green fantasy

1 oz vodka
1 oz dry vermouth
¾ oz Midori melon liqueur
2 tsp fresh lime juice
ice

Pour all ingredients into shaker, shake, then strain into serving glass.

glass 3 oz cocktail glass

garnish lime wheel, strawberries
and mint leaves

left *from left, blue balalaika, green fantasy*

midori-based

japanese slipper

1 oz Midori melon liqueur
1 oz vodka
1 oz fresh lemon juice
ice

Pour all ingredients into shaker, shake, then strain into serving glass.

glass 5 oz champagne saucer

garnish lemon slice

brandy-based

brandy crusta

1 oz brandy
¹/₂ oz maraschino
1 oz fresh orange juice
dash Angostura bitters

Rub rim of serving glass with orange slice then dip into sugar to coat rim. Pour all ingredients into shaker, shake, then strain into serving glass.

glass 5 oz champagne flute

garnish orange slice and cherry

stinger

1¹/₂ oz brandy
¹/₂ white crème de menthe
ice

Pour all ingredients into mixing glass filled with ice, stir, then strain into serving glass.

glass 3 oz cocktail glass

garnish none

left *japanese slipper*

left from left,
brandy crusta, stinger
(recipes previous page)

79

brandy-based

sidecar

1 oz brandy
1 oz Cointreau
1 oz fresh lemon juice
ice

Pour all ingredients into shaker, shake, then strain into serving glass.

glass 3 oz cocktail glass

garnish lemon twist

between the sheets

1 oz brandy
1 oz light rum
1 oz Cointreau
1¹/₂ tsp fresh lemon juice
ice

Pour all ingredients into shaker, shake, then strain into serving glass.

glass 5 oz champagne saucer

garnish lemon twist

right between the sheets

below sidecar

champagne-based

champagne cocktail

1 sugar cube
6 drops Angostura bitters
1/2 oz brandy or cognac
chilled champagne

Soak sugar cube with bitters and drop into champagne flute, pour brandy or cognac on top of bitters, then fill with chilled champagne.

glass 5 oz champagne flute

garnish orange slice

bellini

1/2 fresh peach
chilled champagne

Blend 1/2 peach into puree in blender, spoon into serving glass and top with chilled champagne.

glass 5 oz champagne flute

garnish slice of fresh peach

ritz fizz

dash amaretto
dash strained fresh lemon juice
dash blue curaçao
chilled champagne

Pour amaretto, juice and blue curaçao into serving glass and top with chilled champagne.

glass 5 oz champagne flute

garnish float a rose petal on the
surface if desired

left champagne cocktail

right bellini
far right from left, ritz fizz,
sweet martini (recipe over page)

gin-based

martini

1¹/₂ oz gin
¹/₂ oz dry vermouth
ice

Pour all ingredients into mixing glass filled with ice, stir and strain into serving glass.

glass 3 oz cocktail glass

garnish olive or lemon twist

sweet martini

1¹/₂ oz gin
¹/₂ oz rosso vermouth
ice

Pour all ingredients into mixing glass filled with ice, stir and strain into serving glass.

glass 3 oz cocktail glass

garnish red cherry

right martini

gin-based

gimlet

1¹/₂ oz gin
¹/₂ oz Rose's lime juice
ice

Pour all ingredients into mixing glass filled with ice, stir, then strain into serving glass.

glass 3 oz cocktail glass

garnish lemon twist

after one

³/₄ oz gin
³/₄ oz Galliano
³/₄ oz bianco vermouth
³/₄ oz Campari
ice

Pour all ingredients into mixing glass filled with ice, stir, then strain into serving glass.

glass 3 oz cocktail glass

garnish maraschino cherry and an orange twist

gibson

2 oz gin
1 tsp dry vermouth
ice

Pour all ingredients into mixing glass filled with ice, stir, then strain into serving glass.

glass 3 oz cocktail glass

garnish white cocktail onion

left *from left, gimlet, after one, gibson*

gin-based

1 oz gin
1/2 oz peach brandy
1/2 oz lemon juice
1 egg white
ice

Pour all ingredients into shaker filled with ice, shake, then strain into serving glass.

glass 3 oz champagne saucer

garnish peach slice

3/4 oz gin
3/4 oz medium sherry
3/4 oz rosso vermouth
3/4 oz dry vermouth
1 1/2 tsp Grand Marnier
ice

Pour all ingredients into mixing glass filled with ice, stir, then strain into serving glass.

glass 5 oz champagne saucer

garnish orange spiral and a cherry

left perfect lady
below bartender

gin-based

gin & it

1 oz gin
1 oz bianco vermouth
ice

Pour all ingredients into mixing glass filled with ice, stir, then strain into serving glass.

glass 3 oz cocktail glass

garnish red cherry

victoria

1 oz gin
1 oz dry vermouth
3/4 oz apricot brandy
ice
1 tsp grenadine

Pour gin, dry vermouth and apricot brandy into mixing glass filled with ice, stir, then strain into serving glass. Drop grenadine through the center of the drink.

glass 3 oz cocktail glass

garnish stemmed maraschino cherry

the filby

1 oz gin
1/2 oz amaretto
1/2 oz Campari
1/2 oz dry vermouth
ice

Pour all ingredients into mixing glass filled with ice, stir, then strain into serving glass.

glass 3 oz cocktail glass

garnish orange twist

left from left, gin & it, victoria, the filby

pink gin

dash Angostura bitters
1 1/2 oz gin
1 oz water (optional)

Coat inside of wine goblet with bitters, add chilled gin then cold water if desired.

glass 3 oz cocktail glass

garnish none

blue riband

1 oz gin
1 oz white curaçao
1/2 oz blue curaçao
ice

Pour all ingredients into mixing glass filled with ice, stir, then strain into serving glass.

glass 3 oz cocktail glass

garnish orange twist and a cherry

evergreen

1 oz gin
1/2 oz dry vermouth
1/2 oz Midori melon liqueur
ice
1 1/2 tsp blue curaçao

Pour gin, dry vermouth and Midori melon liqueur into mixing glass filled with ice, stir, then strain into serving glass. Drop blue curacao through the center of the drink.

glass 3 oz cocktail glass

garnish maraschino cherry

left from left, pink gin, blue riband,
evergreen (recipes previous page)

right   from left,
french 75,
dunk cocktail,
clover club
(recipes over page)

gin-based

french 75

1/2 oz gin
1/2 oz fresh lemon juice
1/2 oz sugar syrup
ice
chilled champagne

Pour gin, lemon juice, sugar syrup and ice into shaker, shake, then strain into serving glass. Top with champagne.

glass 5 oz champagne flute

garnish lemon twist and
a maraschino cherry

dunk cocktail

2 oz gin
1 oz dry vermouth
3/4 oz Galliano
2 tsp blue curaçao
ice

Pour all ingredients into mixing glass filled with ice, stir, then strain into serving glass.

glass 5 oz champagne saucer

garnish maraschino cherry

clover club

2 oz gin
1/2 oz fresh lemon juice
1/2 oz grenadine
1/2 egg white
ice

Pour all ingredients into shaker, shake, then strain into serving glass.

glass 5 oz champagne saucer

garnish lemon slices

right from left, bacardi cocktail, daiquiri

light-rum-based

bacardi cocktail

1 oz light rum
1/2 oz fresh lemon juice
1 1/2 tsp grenadine
egg white (optional)
ice

Pour all ingredients into shaker, shake, then strain into serving glass.

glass 3 oz cocktail glass

garnish maraschino cherry

daiquiri

1 1/2 oz light rum
1 oz fresh lemon juice
1/2 oz sugar syrup
egg white (optional)
ice

Pour all ingredients into shaker, shake, then strain into serving glass.

glass 5 oz champagne saucer

garnish lemon slice

apricot lady

1 oz light rum
1 oz apricot brandy
1/2 oz orange curaçao
1/2 oz fresh lime juice
1/2 egg white
ice

Pour all ingredients into blender, blend until smooth, then pour into serving glass.

glass 6 oz old-fashioned

garnish orange slice and a maraschino cherry

banana daiquiri

1 oz light rum
1 oz fresh lemon juice
1 oz sugar syrup
3/4 fresh banana
ice

Pour all ingredients into blender, blend until smooth, then pour into serving glass.

glass 5 oz champagne saucer

garnish slice of banana and mint leaves

left from left, apricot lady,
banana daiquiri
(recipes previous page)

tequila-based

olé

1 oz tequila
1 oz Lena banana liqueur
ice
1½ tsp blue curaçao

Pour tequila and banana liqueur into mixing glass filled with ice, stir, then strain into serving glass. Drop blue curaçao through center of cocktail to achieve a two-tone effect. The blue curaçao will sink because it is heavier than the other ingredients.

glass 3 oz cocktail glass

garnish lime wheel

margarita

1 oz tequila
½ oz fresh lime juice
1 oz Triple Sec or Cointreau
egg white (optional)
ice

Rub rim of glass with lime slice, then dip in salt to coat rim. Pour all ingredients into shaker, shake, then strain into serving glass.

glass 5 oz champagne saucer

garnish lime slice

left olé
below margarita

whisky-based

whisky sour

1¹/₂ oz whisky
1 oz fresh lemon juice
¹/₂ oz sugar syrup
¹/₂ egg white (optional)

Pour all ingredients into shaker, shake,
then strain into serving glass.

glass 6 oz wine-stemmed goblet

garnish maraschino cherry at bottom
of glass, lemon slice on side of glass

right whisky sour

whisky-based

blood & sand

1 oz scotch whisky
1 oz rosso vermouth
1 oz cherry brandy
1 oz orange juice
ice

Pour all ingredients into shaker, shake, then strain into serving glass.

glass 5 oz champagne saucer

garnish orange spiral and a cherry

rob roy

1 oz scotch whisky
1 oz rosso vermouth
dash Angostura bitters
ice

Pour all ingredients into mixing glass filled with ice, stir, then strain into serving glass.

glass 3 oz cocktail glass

garnish maraschino cherry

left blood & sand

right rob roy

whiskey-based

manhattan

1¹/₂ oz rye whiskey
¹/₂ oz rosso vermouth
dash Angostura bitters
ice

Pour all ingredients into mixing glass
filled with ice, stir, then strain into
serving glass.

glass 3 oz cocktail glass

garnish maraschino cherry

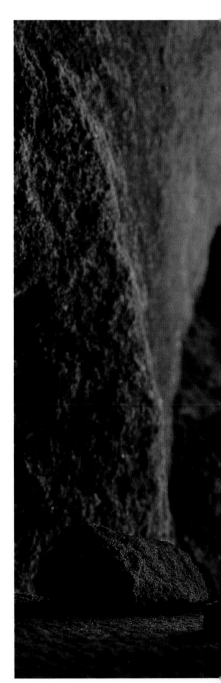

galliano-based

galliano mist

1 oz Galliano
lemon peel slice
  (shaken with ingredients)
ice

Pour all ingredients into shaker, shake,
then pour into serving glass.

glass 6 oz old-fashioned

garnish none

left manhattan

below galliano mist

grand-marnier-based

gloom chaser

1 oz Grand Marnier
1 oz orange curaçao
1 oz lemon juice
1¹/₂ tsp grenadine
ice

Pour all ingredients into shaker, shake,
then strain into serving glass.

glass 5 oz champagne saucer

garnish orange twist

lena-banana-liqueur-based

the ripper

³/₄ oz Lena banana liqueur
³/₄ oz Peachtree liqueur
¹/₂ oz fresh lemon juice
³/₄ oz dry vermouth
ice
1¹/₂ tsp blue curaçao

Pour Lena banana liqueur, Peachtree liqueur,
juice and dry vermouth into shaker with ice,
shake, then strain into serving glass. Drop
blue curaçao through center of drink.

glass 3 oz cocktail glass

garnish lemon wheel and mint leaves

cognac-based

happy world

¹/₂ oz cognac
1 oz Cointreau
1 oz orange juice
¹/₂ oz banana liqueur

Pour all ingredients into shaker, shake,
then strain into serving glass.

glass 5 oz champagne saucer

garnish orange slice and a cherry

right from left, gloom chaser,
the ripper, happy world

crème-de-cassis-based

kir royale

1 tsp crème de cassis
chilled champagne

Pour crème de cassis into serving glass
and top with champagne.

glass 5 oz champagne flute

garnish none

kir

1/2 oz crème de cassis
chilled dry white wine

Pour crème de cassis into serving glass
and top with white wine.

glass 5 oz wine goblet

garnish none

left kir royale   *right* kir

nightcaps

Drift off with these sublime nightcaps.
Spice up the coffee with some
Irish whiskey and a cloud of cream
or dispense with it all together and
try a Hot Buttered Rum, a Scotch
Mist or a Grand Marnier Fireball.
Sweet dreams.

grand-marnier-based

grand marnier fireball

1 oz Grand Marnier
1 oz cognac
orange wedge

Pour ingredients into a warm brandy balloon, ignite and add orange wedge. Let flame for about 15 seconds, then extinguish and inhale fumes while glass is cooling.

glass 10 oz brandy balloon

garnish none

amaretto-based

p.s. I love you

1 oz amaretto
1 oz Kahlua
1 oz Baileys Irish Cream
ice

Pour all ingredients, one on top of the other, over ice in serving glass and stir with a swizzle stick.

glass 6 oz old-fashioned

garnish sprinkle of nutmeg

right grand marnier fireball

below p.s. i love you

whisky-based

rusty nail

1¹/₂ oz scotch whisky
³/₄ oz Drambuie
ice

Pour ingredients, one on top of the
other, over ice in serving glass.

glass 6 oz old-fashioned

garnish lemon twist

hot toddy

2 oz scotch whisky
   (or any preferred spirit or liqueur)
1 teaspoon honey or brown sugar
boiling water

Pour whisky into serving glass,
add honey or sugar then top with
boiling water.

glass 5 oz wine goblet

garnish lemon slice studded with
cloves, a cinnamon stick and
a sprinkle of nutmeg

right hot toddy

below rusty nail

whisky-based

blue blazer

2 oz scotch whisky
2 oz boiling water
1/2 oz sugar syrup

Pour scotch into silver goblet, combine boiling water and sugar syrup in another goblet. Ignite scotch and gently pour on top of boiling water. Pour back and forth between goblets to mix.

glasses two silver goblets or heatproof glasses

garnish lemon twist

scotch mist

1 oz scotch whisky
twist of lemon
ice

Pour all ingredients into shaker, shake, then pour into serving glass.

glass 6 oz old-fashioned

garnish none

left blue blazer
below scotch mist

rum-based

hot buttered rum

1 small slice butter
1 teaspoon brown sugar
cinnamon
nutmeg
vanilla extract
1 oz dark rum
boiling water

Mix butter, brown sugar, cinnamon, nutmeg and vanilla until creamed. Place one teaspoon into a serving glass, pour dark rum and boiling water into serving glass and mix well.

glass 6 oz stemmed wine goblet

garnish none

hot eggnog

1/2 oz dark rum
1/2 oz brandy
1½ tsp sugar syrup
1 egg
hot milk

Pour rum, brandy, sugar syrup and egg into blender, blend for about 30 seconds then pour into serving glass. Top with hot milk and mix well.

glass 10 oz highball

garnish nutmeg

left hot buttered rum

right hot eggnog

vodka-based

black russian

ice
1 oz vodka
1 oz Kahlua
cola top up (optional)

Place a scoop of crushed ice in serving glass. Pour vodka then Kahlua into glass. Top up with cola if desired.

glass 6 oz old-fashioned

garnish none

wine-based

glühwein

1 bottle red wine
3 tablespoons sugar
2 slices lemon
2 slices orange
1 cinnamon stick

Warm all ingredients in a saucepan until very hot. Do not boil. Serve in a heated goblet.

glass 5 oz wine goblet

garnish none

irish-whiskey-based

irish coffee

1 teaspoon brown sugar
1 oz Irish whiskey
4 oz hot black coffee
fresh cream

Put sugar into the bottom of serving glass and cover with Irish whiskey. Top with coffee and mix well. Float cold cream on the surface by pouring it into a teaspoon and letting it overflow onto the surface of the drink.

glass irish coffee glass

garnish grated chocolate

right glühwein

below black russian

right *irish coffee*
(recipe previous page)

garnishes

Choose fruit that is firm, unblemished and has a good color. Wash fruit just before use.

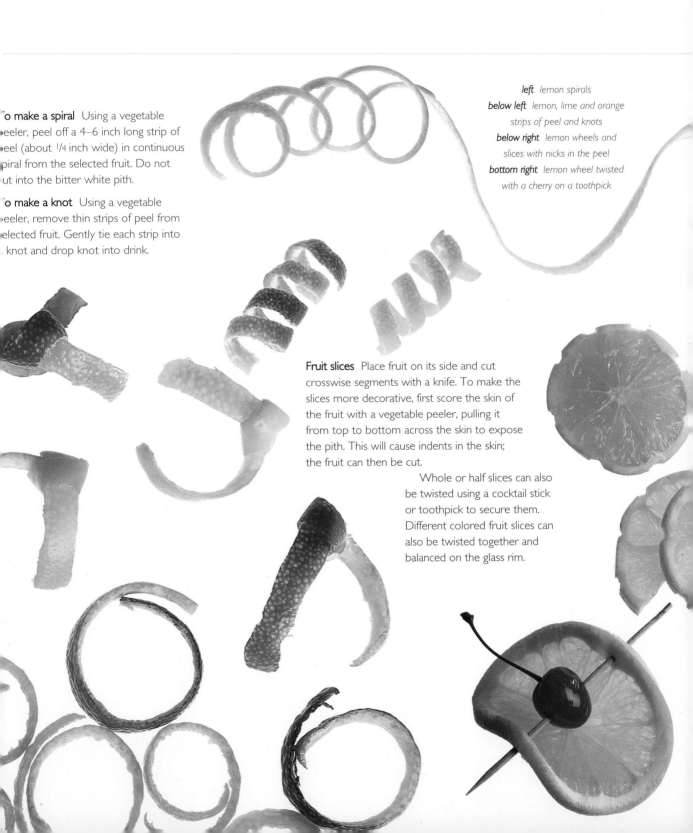

To make a spiral Using a vegetable peeler, peel off a 4–6 inch long strip of peel (about 1/4 inch wide) in continuous spiral from the selected fruit. Do not cut into the bitter white pith.

To make a knot Using a vegetable peeler, remove thin strips of peel from selected fruit. Gently tie each strip into a knot and drop knot into drink.

left lemon spirals
below left lemon, lime and orange strips of peel and knots
below right lemon wheels and slices with nicks in the peel
bottom right lemon wheel twisted with a cherry on a toothpick

Fruit slices Place fruit on its side and cut crosswise segments with a knife. To make the slices more decorative, first score the skin of the fruit with a vegetable peeler, pulling it from top to bottom across the skin to expose the pith. This will cause indents in the skin; the fruit can then be cut.

Whole or half slices can also be twisted using a cocktail stick or toothpick to secure them. Different colored fruit slices can also be twisted together and balanced on the glass rim.

Strawberries Choose firm ripe strawberries with nice green-leafed tops. Cut strawberry in half lengthwise. For more elaborate decoration, make several cuts lengthwise into the strawberry's flesh to form a fan.

Bananas Choose firm unblemished fruit and prepare just before serving. Cut unpeeled bananas into slices, dip in lemon juice to prevent discoloration. Make a cut into center of slice and balance on glass rim. Pair with a cherry or other colorful fruit.

left strawberry fan
right strawberry, pineapple leaves ar
lemon piece on a toothpic

Melons Use a melon scoop to remove balls from different types of melons. Spear balls on a toothpick and use as a garnish.

Fresh coconut Crack coconut shell with hammer. Pare off thin peelings of coconut with a sharp knife. These will curl up and can be used on top of the drink, or on glass rim. Alternatively, grate coconut flesh and sprinkle on top of drink.

Pineapple Leaves from head of pineapple can be sliced in the center at the bottom of the leaf and placed on the rim of a glass or skewered on a toothpick and placed in the drink. Slices of pineapple, cut either in quarters, halves or eighths can also be used with the leaves.

above banana slices
below honeydew melon
and cantaloupe balls
on a toothpick

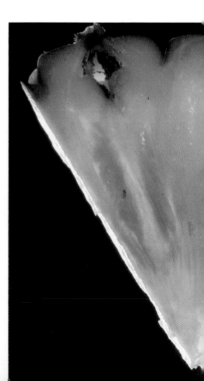

above *pineapple half with leaves and a cherry on a toothpick*
right *nutmeg sprinkled as a topping*
below *coconut frosting and a pineapple piece*

Frostings

Glasses can be dipped in salt, lightly beaten egg white, sugar, coconut or instant coffee or cocoa. Remember to rub the rim with lemon or orange first. Water will just dissolve the frosting.

Toppings

Freshly grated whole nutmeg, freshly ground cinnamon, freshly ground coffee beans or instant coffee, grated chocolate or chocolate curls (made by pulling the blade of a sharp knife or a vegetable peeler along a block of chocolate).

fruit

Many fruits are easily blended and add color, flavor and texture to drinks.
The fruits listed below are the most suitable for mixed drinks.

Apples Do not blend apples, use apple juice instead.

Apricots Firm and juicy when ripe, canned apricots are also suitable after they have been drained.

Avocados Produce thick drinks when blended with cream.

Bananas A strong tasting fruit, the banana must be blended until smooth. Adding crème de banane to a cocktail with fresh banana will make it sweeter.

Cherries Canned cherries are the most suitable as they have the stones removed. Maraschino cherries are used for decorating cocktails.

Grapefruit Has a tangy citrus flavor.

Lemon Balances the sugar-level of cocktails and is best used freshly-squeezed.

Limes Have a sweet-sour taste. Lime cordial can also be used and will sweeten a drink.

Mandarins Very juicy fruit with a subtle flavor; segments can be used as decoration.

Mangoes Have a very distinctive flavor and aroma. They must be very ripe and will thicken a drink. Mango nectar can be substituted but will not provide the same texture as the fresh fruit.

Melons Add body to a drink but do not have a very strong flavor.

Oranges Sometimes the skins are added to drinks; unsweetened juice can be substituted for freshly-squeezed oranges.

Passionfruit A very sweet fruit which can be used in blended drinks; bottled passionfruit can also be substituted.

Peaches Must be peeled before blending; canned peaches can be used and will add a sweeter flavor to the drink.

Pears Must be carefully handled so as not to bruise; must be peeled before blending; canned pears can be substituted.

Pineapples A very sweet fruit that must be used ripe; canned slices can be used

but are sweeter than the fresh fruit. The juice as well as the fruit is used in many cocktails.

Raspberries Ripe fruit add color and texture to a drink, they can be frozen and blended; raspberries will keep in the refrigerator for a few days.

Strawberries Must be washed so as not to give a gritty taste, they add good color and flavor.

right peach halves are blended to give a peach marnier *its distinct flavor, page 56*

liqueurs

There are thousands of liqueurs available throughout the world, some are fruit-based, others herb-based and others still are plant- and nut-based. Monks and physicians were the first to mix these exotic ingredients which they originally used for healing purposes.

In the 1500s, the Italians began mixing these potions and drinking them for pleasure. Fruit liqueurs resulted because much of the fruit harvested in the summer had to be preserved for winter.

We have listed some of the more common liqueurs and their ingredients.

Fruit-based liqueurs

Apricot One of the most popular fruit liqueurs, it is made from softening apricot flesh in brandy.

Banana The best of these liqueurs have a light color and a strong smell of ripe bananas. The most popular is crème de bananes, which is made from a maceration of bananas in spirit.

Blackberry The brandy flavored with blackberry juice has low alcoholic content and a fruity sweet taste, whereas that distilled from blackberries has a dry flavor and a high alcoholic content.

Blackcurrant Cassis is the name given to this fruit-based liqueur which results from blackcurrants being softened in spirit (usually brandy) for about two months. When this liquid is mixed with sugar and distilled it produces crème de cassis. Cassis will take on a brownish tinge if exposed to air for too long.

Cherry Cherries are pressed, the juice is extracted then mixed with brandy. Maraschino is made by crushing the cherries and stones, then distilling and sweetening the liquid.

Coconut Formed by softening coconut flesh in light rum.

Melon One of the new style of liqueurs, this liquid has a very sweet flavor. Midori is the widely known brand.

Orange These liqueurs are known as curaçaos and come in a variety of styles such as dry and bitter. They are made from grape spirit, sugar and orange peel. Southern Comfort is flavored with oranges and peaches.

Peach This liqueur is produced from peaches which are matured in brandy with other juices.

Raspberry This soft fruit is soaked in spirit to produce crème de framboise. When it is distilled, a dry tasting, colorless spirit called framboise results.

Strawberry Crème de fraises is a liqueur flavored with strawberries. Crème de fraises de bois is a liqueur produced from wild strawberries.

Herb-based liqueurs

Benedictine This very sweet liqueur has a strong herb aroma and is amber colored. It was first made by the monks of the Benedictine monastery at Fecamp in Normandy.

Chartreuse This liqueur has been produced by the monks of La Grande Chartreuse monastery for more than 300 years. The potent green liqueur has a pungent herby taste, while the yellow Chartreuse is sweeter and less alcoholic.

Drambuie This liqueur is based on Scotch malt whisky that has been flavored with honey and herbs.

Galliano An Italian liqueur with a lemon-aniseed flavor and golden color. It is sold in tall flute-shaped bottles.

Irish Mist Originating in Ireland, this liqueur is based on whisky and heather honey.

Sambuca Witch elderbush and licorice are the major components of this Italian liqueur. A popular way of drinking it is with three coffee beans set alight on top; this adds a "toasted" flavor to the drink.

Plant- and nut-based liqueurs

Almond This liqueur is made from bitter almonds and the crushed stones of fruits. The most popular of today's almond liqueurs is amaretto, which also contains apricots.

Anise One of the oldest known flavorings. Anise is the base of this liqueur. It has a taste like licorice. Aniseed drinks turn cloudy when mixed with water.

Chocolate This liqueur is flavored with roasted cacao beans and is known as crème de cacao.

Coffee Coffee liqueur, crème de mocca and crème de café are made from coffee beans which have been soaked and percolated.

Mint These liqueurs have a tangy aroma and are made by crushing oil from the mint leaves. Mint liqueurs successfully capture the heady aroma and refreshing taste of mint.

glossary

Advocaat A Dutch liqueur made from egg yolks, sugar and brandy.

Amaretto An Italian liqueur with an almond-apricot base.

Anisette A very sweet, colorless, aniseed-flavored liqueur.

Apricot brandy A highly flavored liqueur made from apricots.

Benedictine A sweet herb-flavored, brandy-based liqueur.

Bitters Made up of aromatics, contains roots and herbs and is used for flavor.

Blackberry brandy A dark liqueur flavored with blackberries.

Blackberry liqueur Also known as cassis, contains blackcurrants, brandy and sugar.

Boilermaker A shot of straight whisky followed by a beer chaser.

Bourbon An American whisky made from grain and aged in charred oak barrels. At least 51% corn.

Brandy Distilled from fermented juices of ripe grapes and other fruits.

Campari An Italian aperitif with a strong bitter taste.

Champagne A light sparkling wine, usually white; traditionally from the famous Champagne district in France.

Chartreuse A liqueur which contains more than 130 spices and herbs. There are two types; yellow which is light, and the green which is heavier and stronger in spirit strength.

Cherry brandy A liqueur made from the juice of cherries and brandy.

Chianti A dry Italian wine; mostly red, but some white is available.

Cognac Brandy from the Cognac region in France.

Cointreau A sweet, colorless, orange-flavored liqueur.

Crème de banane A brandy-based, banana-flavored liqueur.

Crème de cacao A sweet, dark liqueur made from cocoa beans, vanilla and spices. Has a cocoa flavor.

Crème de cassis A liqueur with a blackcurrant flavor.

Crème de fraises A sweet liqueur with a strawberry flavor.

Crème de frambiose A sweet liqueur with a raspberry flavor.

Crème de menthe A peppermint-flavored liqueur. Available in white, green and red.

Curaçao A sweet liqueur made from wine or grape spirit, sugar and orange peel. Available in orange, white, green and blue.

Drambuie A liqueur based on Scotch and heather honey.

Dubonnet A dark red aperitif wine with a slight quinine taste.

Galliano A gold-colored liqueur with a licorice and aniseed flavor.

Gin A distillation of grain with a juniper berry flavor.

Glayva Scottish liqueur similar to Drambuie.

Goldwasser A colorless sweet liqueur with gold flakes flavored with orange and aniseed.

Grand Marnier A golden-brown French brandy liqueur with an orange flavor.

Green ginger wine Wine made from fruit and Jamaican ginger.

Grenadine A red non-alcoholic sugar syrup used for sweetness.

Kahlua A Mexican coffee liqueur made from cocoa beans, coffee beans, vanilla and brandy.

Kirsch A colorless fruit brandy distilled from black cherries.

Kummel A colorless liqueur flavored with caraway seeds and cumin.

Maraschino A colorless Italian cherry-flavored liqueur.

Midori A Japanese honeydew melon liqueur, lime green in color.

Ouzo A Greek liqueur with an aniseed flavor.

Parfait Amour A highly scented French liqueur made from lemons, oranges, brandy and herbs. Light purple in color.

Peach brandy A liqueur with a peach flavor.

Pernod A French aperitif. Pernod 45 has an aniseed flavor. Pernod Pastis has a licorice flavor.

Pimms No 1 has a gin base. No 2 has a whisky base. No 3 has a brandy base. No 6 has a vodka base.

Rum A distillation of molasses from crushed sugar cane. Color can vary from light to dark.

Sabra A liqueur with a chocolate and orange flavor.

Sambuca An Italian liqueur with a soft anisette flavor.

Southern Comfort An American liqueur with a brandy and bourbon base and a peach flavour.

Sugar syrup A mixture of equal parts white sugar and water. Boil mixture until sugar is dissolved. Can be stored in refrigerator indefinitely.

Tequila A colorless spirit made from the fermented juice of a cactus plant from Mexico, the agave or mescal.

Tia Maria A Jamaican liqueur based on rum. Has a coffee flavor.

Toddy A mixture of spirit and hot water

Triple Sec White curaçao, see curaçao.

Vermouth A wine fortified with herbs.

Vodka A colorless and almost tasteless distillation of grain.

Wine Usually the fermented juice of grapes.

Whisky A distillation of grain, malt, sugar and yeast. Also Irish whiskey and rye whiskey.

index